Shelter

Susan Canizares • Daniel Moreton

Scholastic Inc.

New York • Toronto • London • Auckland • Sydney

Acknowledgments

Literacy Specialist: Linda Cornwell

Social Studies Consultant: Barbara Schubert, Ph.D.

Design: Silver Editions

Photo Research: Silver Editions

Endnotes: Jacqueline Smith

Endnote Illustrations: Anthony Carnabucia

———————————————

Photographs: Cover: John Beatty/Tony Stone Images; p. 1: (tl) John Beatty/Tony Stone Images; (tr) Pete Saloutos/The Stock Market; (bl) George Ancona/International Stock Photography; (br) S. R. Maglione/Photo Researchers Inc.; p. 2: Rafael Macia/Photo Researchers Inc.; p. 3: Grant Heilman/Grant Heilman Photography, Inc.; p. 4: Sylvain Grandadam/Tony Stone Images; p. 5: Michael Howell/Envision; p. 6: 91RB Studio/The Stock Market; p. 7: Jeff Greenberg/Photo Researchers Inc.; p. 8: David R. Frazier/Photo Researchers Inc.; p. 9: Michael Ventura/International Stock Photography; p. 10: Craig Aurness/Woodfin Camp & Assoc., Inc.; p. 11: Chris Bonington/International Stock Photography; p. 12: W. Hill, Jr./The Image Works.

Library of Congress Cataloging-in-Publication Data
Canizares, Susan, 1960-
Shelter/Susan Canizares, Daniel Moreton.
p.cm.--(Social studies emergent readers)
Summary: Photographs and simple text describe some of the different kinds of structures that people call home, from houseboats and clay huts to farmhouses and apartment buildings.
ISBN 0-439-04550-9 (pbk.: alk. paper)
1. Dwellings--Juvenile literature. 2. Architecture, Domestic--Juvenile literature.
3. Architecture and climate--Juvenile literature. [1. Dwellings. 2. Architecture, Domestic.]
I. Moreton, Daniel. II. Title. III. Series.
GT171.C36 1998
392.3'6--dc21   98-53115
                                                                                                                CIP AC

10   08   03   02

A shelter is a place to live.

It can be a lighthouse

or a houseboat.

It can be a clay hut

or an adobe.

It can be a skyscraper

or a townhouse.

It can be a farmhouse

or a log cabin.

You can live in a shelter for a long time

or a short time.

A shelter is a home.

Shelter

Shelter is a basic human need. It protects us from bad weather, harsh sun, and extreme cold. Shelter provides safety from dangerous animals and enemies. We eat, sleep, raise children, and keep our belongings in shelters. Shelters are homes. People build shelters everywhere: in the desert, in the city, even on the water. The types of shelter people build depend on their surroundings, the available building materials, and their way of life.

Lighthouse Lighthouses make navigation safer and easier in harbors and ports. Without their powerful beacons—and the sound of their foghorns when it's too foggy to see—sea captains traveling at night or in a storm might not be aware of dangerous rocks or shallow waters. There would be many more shipwrecks. Some lighthouses are very ancient. In Alexandria, Egypt, a giant stone lighthouse 40 stories high was built in 280 B.C. It guided ships for 1,000 years and was known as one of the Seven Wonders of the World.

Houseboat A houseboat is a shelter on the water. Houseboats are one way to find shelter in overcrowded cities. They are very common in many of the world's big cities that have canals or rivers flowing through them. Houseboats are designed for living rather than for moving and are not usually constructed for long-distance travel.

Skyscrapers and townhouses In cities there is not enough land to build houses for all the people. The only way to provide enough shelter for everyone is to build upward. The invention of the elevator and steel frames (strong, but lighter than brick or stone) made skyscrapers possible. The Sears Tower in Chicago, built in 1973, is the tallest building in the United States. It stands 1,454 feet high and has 110 floors!

Clay huts and adobe The desert is very dry and windy. For most of the year it is very hot during the day and cool at night. Shelters in the desert need thick walls to keep out the heat during the day and keep people warm at night. Clay huts, called hogans, have only one room, with a hole in the roof to let out smoke from the fire used for cooking and heating. The Navajos, Native Americans who live in the Southwest, use logs to build a circular frame and then cover it with a thick layer of clay, which bakes hard in the sun. This material is called adobe.

Farmhouses Today most people live in or around cities, but for thousands of years many people lived in the country. Farmhouses are homes in places where people raise animals and grow crops. They are made of wood or stone and often have several separate buildings with different functions. Animals live in the barn, and grain is stored in the silo.

Log cabins Another kind of shelter in the country is the log cabin. German and Swedish settlers introduced this kind of house to the U.S., and it became very popular in the West because it was easy to build and the materials were easy to find. The settlers chopped down the trees, put the logs one on top of the other, and used grass or mud to fill in the holes between the logs.

For a long time or a short time Most people live in solid shelters of brick, wood, stone, or steel, which stand for many, many years. But some people are nomads—they travel around from place to place and live in tents, mobile homes, or houseboats. Other people leave their permanent homes for part of the year and use temporary shelters. The Inuits of the frozen Arctic regions used to live in temporary shelters called igloos when they went hunting in the winter. An Inuit could build an igloo for overnight shelter in an hour, but sometimes they built several larger igloos, connected by passageways, where families lived for several months. In the summer the igloos would melt and the Inuits would move to other kinds of shelters. Today most Inuits live in modern housing.